SM/

SCATTERED TEENS

Executive functioning skills to set goals, improve focus, manage emotions, get organized, and live your dream life + workbook

Lauren Douglas

Legal & Disclaimer

The content and information in this book are consistent and truthful, and it has been provided for informational, educational, and business purposes only.

Table of Contents

Free Bonus eBooks for my readers

Dear Reader,

I wanted to personally thank you for choosing my book as your guide to navigating through the challenges of adolescence and beyond. It's an honor to be part of your journey toward developing the essential skills for success.

As a parent and educator, I've seen firsthand the struggles that teenagers face in this modern world. The pressures of academics, social media, and the constant stream of distractions can make it difficult to stay on track. That's why I wrote this book - to provide a comprehensive guide to help teenagers improve their executive functioning skills, including planning, organization, time management, and self-regulation.

I hope that the strategies and techniques outlined in this book will help you or your teenager to stay focused and motivated and achieve success in all areas of life. As a bonus, I would like to offer you two additional eBooks.

"Distractions in The Digital Era"
A practical and concise book that provides actionable strategies for effectively managing distractions in the modern world. With insights on the latest digital tools and techniques, this guide empowers readers to regain focus and productivity, reduce stress and overwhelm, and reclaim their time and energy.

"Master Your Self-Discipline & Self-Motivation"

A practical guide that helps readers to cultivate the habits and mindset needed to achieve their goals. This book offers strategies to overcome procrastination, manage distractions, and stay focused on what truly matters. Readers will be empowered to create lasting change in their lives and achieve success in any area they choose to pursue.

To get these books, just scan this QR Code:

Sincerely, Lauren Douglas

Introduction

As a teenager, you are navigating a complex and demanding world. Many challenges require strong executive functioning skills, from balancing schoolwork, extracurricular activities, and social life to managing time, emotions, and stress. Executive functioning is a set of mental skills that help you plan, organize, prioritize, and execute tasks effectively. It encompasses critical abilities like working memory, inhibitory control, and cognitive flexibility, which are essential for success in school, work, and life.

This book is designed to help teens like you understand the importance of executive functioning and how to develop these skills to reach your full potential. Whether you struggle with organization, planning, or time management, or want to improve your cognitive skills, this book offers practical strategies and activities to help you achieve your goals.

You may feel overwhelmed and uncertain about developing your executive functioning skills, but you are not alone. Many teens struggle with similar challenges, but you can overcome them with the proper support and guidance. This book will give you an overview of the critical components of executive functioning, how they impact daily life, and how to identify and assess any executive functioning deficits.

This book will teach you how to develop your executive functioning skills through various effective strategies and activities. From taking notes and creating flashcards to incorporating physical exercise and mindfulness into your daily routine, you will discover a range of apps/roaches that can help you improve your cognitive skills. This book will guide you through identifying and assessing your executive functioning deficits and provide tips and techniques for overcoming them.

You will also learn how improved executive functioning skills can positively impact different areas of your life, from academics and social interactions to time management and stress management.

With real-life examples and case studies, you will see how other teens have successfully developed their executive functioning skills and how it has improved their lives.

With this guide, you have access to a personalized workbook section and worksheets that allow you plan and track your progress. There is also a **NOTES** section to write things down, so you don't forget.

If you are ready to take control of your cognitive skills and reach your full potential, this book is for you.

With its comprehensive approach and practical tips, you will be on your way to becoming a confident and capable young adult.

Chapter 1: General Overview of Executive Functioning

Have you ever wondered why the confusion, change, high emotions, and impulsive decision-making characterize your teenage period? You've got a lot of ideas running through your mind, yet you need help to grab one and implement it. It is now looking like you will fail academically or fail to perform as you ought to socially. I understand the pain, but you don't have to feel bad about that. Do you know why? Around five out of ten teenagers experience the same issue. So, you are not facing a distinct issue, but one common to people in their teenage years. This is because of executive function skills. These skills need to evolve as you grow; you will be able to handle tasks (complex or simple) better the further you go into adulthood. You can call this a mental developmental process that your frontal lobe must pass through so you can fit into the 'real world'. Your brain needs to pass through this stage, as it is typical that a teenager's ability to make decisions is often dictated by 'gut' instincts rather than rational and critical reasoning.

Some people know about executive functioning skills as they relate to disabilities in learning. What seems obscure to many people, especially teenagers, is that no child is born with inherent executive functioning skills. A lack of these skills in a teenager's life produces symptoms of ADHD and ADD.

Have you ever thought of that?

Perhaps you have seen teenagers who perform at the peak of their academic capabilities, and you thought they were born with those executive functioning skills. That's not so. Instead, these skills are learned and refined throughout adolescence and into adulthood. At this stage of your life, your prefrontal cortex, which governs most of these skills, is undergoing a developmental process. The environment you create to enhance this growth is essential to perform better academically.

However, before learning how this occurs, we must discuss what executive functioning is, how this term relates to the skills you need to succeed in school, and how you can build these skills as you grow. Knowing this is a vital step in optimizing your organizational skills.

What is executive Functioning, exactly?

Right now, I want your mind to transfer quickly to your studies. The best way to get the gist of what executive functioning means is to look around you and observe your activities. By activities I mean, planning, organizing, and solving problems. You read books, work on your assignments, and do chores. All these activities involve planning, working memory, and organization.

It is nearly impossible to demonstrate one of these skills without the other. You use problem-solving and emotional control skills to navigate difficult situations and complex tasks. That's precisely what executive functioning skills help you to achieve.

Executive Functioning refers to functions that help you manage your life's tasks. These functions are processes that involve managing your life and resources to achieve a particular goal. Word executive functioning is an umbrella team for neurologically-based skills that involve self-regulation and mental control.

Significant Areas of Executive Functioning

According to Harvard University's Center on Developing Children, three brain functions give rise to executive functioning skills.

They are:

- Self-control (inhibitory)
- Mental (cognitive) flexibility
- Working memory

If you are reading this for the first time, I want you to understand that all your activities revolve around these critical brain functions.

Let's start by explaining the first brain function - self-control.

Self-control

This is the most common brain function of all. It centers around your ability to control your behavior, emotions, and impulses to achieve definite and long-term goals. For instance, when you are frustrated because you can't meet your academic grades, rather than expressing yourself using colorful language to your teacher, you use cognitive self-control to neutralize your emotions to improve in this academic term.

Other common instances that rely on cognitive control are:

- Setting and reaching long-term goals
- Tracking and monitoring your progress
- Remaining inspired
- Mental (cognitive) flexibility

Do you remember how you can change your plan or action with little thought?

Mental flexibility is your ability to alter or adjust a plan in response to stimuli.

For example, you are working on an artwork assignment from school and suddenly discover you need more paint. You have to improvise and continue where you stopped without starting all over again. That's exactly how cognitive flexibility works. Your brain always allows changes to occur to anything you have planned, even when you have not considered it. This is also known as the ability to think on your feet.

Other common activities that rely on cognitive flexibility include:

- Learning from your past errors and mistakes
- Tolerating ambiguities
- Reflecting on risks before taking them
- Exploring different means of solving problems
- Viewing things from others' perspectives
- Carefully weigh options before concluding
- Shifting attention from one speaker to another during a lesson or discussion

Working memory

Your working memory is responsible for your ability to retain and use a piece of information for a short time. This working memory allows you to weigh options by using the information available and determine its relevance to what you are doing now.

It also helps you get the latest information that you can use immediately. For example, your working memory helps you to remember where you dropped your school bag during your rush back home. Other common activities that rely on working memory are:

· Maintaining concentration and focus

· Remember your parents' phone numbers after you've dialed for a long time

· Summarizing new information

· Reflect on a word problem long enough to solve it

How Executive Function Skills Develop

EF starts early in life. As you reach the age of maturity, your brain starts to develop, especially as you interact with people such as your teachers, parents, siblings, classmates, and other family members. So, the foundation for the development of executive function is directly associated with the early attachment relationship you have with the adults around you. This shows how healthy your relationship is with these people and how it will reflect on your executive function. Teens with healthy relationships with the adults around them tend to be safe and secure. This sense of security from reliable and trustworthy adults helps them build confidence and high esteem, helping them to conveniently and comfortably explore their world, gain freedom, and solve problems.

More so, secure relationships help to form the basis for solid emotional development and executive function skills in adolescents. Teenagers who develop EF early in life tend to demonstrate high self-control in academic and social environments, mainly as they grow older and transition into secondary school.

As you are now in high school your executive function skills are reflected in most of the things you do. Your ability to set goals, organize your time, follow through with tasks required to achieve these goals, and appropriate the self-reinforcement needed to get you there is vital. These skills are associated with social competence, academic achievement, and overall personal well-being (mental and physical).

Does Executive Functioning impact your academics and personal life?

Students of all ages, from primary school through university must learn many skills to help them navigate through life and school. The truth is, both school and life have challenges that they project on you as you transition from one phase to another. You then need strong skills to tackle these challenges and become a champion. If you struggle with life and academic challenges without executive function, these are the following areas where you are likely to struggle:

Homework - After you've been taught in school, you believe you will attend to your assignment when you get home, but suddenly you can't remember any of the information you have been taught. You will often need help understanding your homework requirements and details again. You may also procrastinate, completely forget about it, or fail to finish it, meaning you arrive at school the next day with incomplete homework.

Grades: Low grades are surprising, but they often don't reflect your ability or potential. Late and missing assignments affect grades. The inability to study when required will also affect your grades.

Planners: When it comes to planning, you don't write anything down, except when you are forced to do so.

You fail to understand short-term planning techniques and, most times, don't plan at all.

Time management: You tend to procrastinate or take longer to complete tasks.

Preparation: Not being fully prepared for classes; absent-minded when you are in class, don't have materials you need; forgetting pen or pencils, books, and homework; not prepared to leave the house for school at the right time.

Organization: Papers, desks, backpacks, and other school materials must be arranged appropriately.

Advocacy: Unwillingness to ask for help. A lack of the understanding that a teacher is a resourceful person, not reading directions carefully, and doesn't attend to assignments on time. Never want to seek help or accept one when others offer to help.

Details: Not noticing essential details about assignments, not hearing teacher expectations on assignments, and jumping to conclusions without paying attention to detail. Never email the teacher when you have questions.

Overwhelm; Most times; you need to figure out where and how to start as you are excessively overwhelmed with details. You tend to procrastinate because you are overwhelmed, resist help from parents, and experience fights at home.

Focus: When you pay little attention to one thing at a time, you do incomplete work because you are easily distracted. Facing problems, trying to stay concentrated, and finding it challenging to stay focused and read a passage effectively.

Writing: Having issues organizing your thoughts and penning them down. Ideas go in countless directions, need help editing correctly, have trouble clarifying ideas, and take more extended time than they should. You can communicate your ideas verbally but experience difficulty in writing them down.

How Can You Build Executive Functioning Skills?

Executive functioning skills need to be practiced throughout high school. Some ways you can develop these skills include:

Have a SMART Goal

SMART goals are not only for adults. As a teenager, you can choose to set goals that challenge you but can be achieved. After choosing them, you write them down, holding yourself accountable and responsible. You can work backward from your end goal to establish a planning process with different, concrete steps toward the finished product. There is every possibility that you will need help. Before the time comes, you should create a check-in process in advance so that your parents or trusted adults around you can provide direction and support and be accountable as you work towards your long-term goal.

Use an Organizer

Having a structure that reminds you of countless commitments, dates, and deadlines is a requirement for success. Think about having a special pen and paper system to assist you in internalizing. Doing that helps you get focused, as writing by hand requires attention and concentration.

Simultaneously, you have an electronic backup system to help provide automated reminders and notify you of your daily schedules and commitments. Combining these two helps maximize your productivity.

Practice self-monitoring

Misunderstandings, negative self-talk, and too many tasks can form roadblocks to your skills, but practicing self-monitoring can help you address all these challenges.

You can start by becoming aware of those underlying negative thoughts. Once you can identify them, you take a step back to see them more objectively. That has to do with recognizing areas for growth rather than areas of failure. Change your thinking pattern to what you will do to get better next time rather than solely reflecting on the negatives and generating a bad vibe. For instance, if you've had a negative discussion with your schoolmate, you can imagine seeing things from their perspective and thinking about what their experience and views might be. This will help give them the benefit of the doubt.

You can also monitor yourself to know your efforts toward recognizing your barriers. If you are constantly falling off-track by engaging in things that easily distract you, then remove these distractions so you can focus on what you need to focus on.

Talk to a mentor

Developing executive functioning skills is not instant and won't happen immediately. You also can't do it alone. The guidance of role models will help make the journey easier. Whether they can help you fine-tune your approach to long-term assignments or studying, provide help in areas where you need to develop, and make you accountable for the goals that you have set for yourself.

To summarize, as a teenager, executive function skills will continue to be essential for you to gain independence, improve your critical thinking skills, set and follow through with goals, and look ahead to your future. As adolescents mature, the adults in their lives (parents and other essential adults) are critical for developing and maintaining this skill.

Key Takeaways

In this chapter; you have learned all, but not limited to, the following;

- Executive Functioning refers to functions that help you manage life's tasks
- Self-control is your ability to control your behavior, emotions, and impulses to achieve definite and long-term goals
- Mental flexibility involves your ability to alter a plan or adjust one in response to stimuli
- Working memory is essential because it allows you to weigh up your options by using the information available to you and determine its relevance to what you are doing at the moment

Chapter 2: Understanding Executive Functioning

Adolescence is a period that ushers in new expectations and responsibilities across all spheres of one's life. Ordinarily, people at this stage leverage these years to build their identities and establish the foundations for a healthy movement into adulthood. In other words, this is the stage you are expected to develop your self-identity and create formidable relationships that transmit into adulthood.

Your brain also grows as you develop your values, perspectives, and identities. The parts of the brain responsible for attention, reasoning, decision-making, and emotional processes are also improving. This process is what I have explained to be 'executive function,' which follows throughout adolescence. Combined with impulsive decisions or risky behavior with common social pressures. When you understand these changes in the brain and the common causes of executive function issues, you, with the help of your mentor or parents, will develop techniques to help you succeed across all areas of your life.

What more is executive function?

As I briefly discussed in the previous chapter, executive functioning involves mental growth. Your brain is expected to grow throughout adolescence. The reason why this is vital is that there are some tasks you need to perform all by yourself, which of course, would require some special abilities or skills. So, when you've taken your time to build them, you will not only be able to cope with your academics and everything that revolves around you but also will mature to be that adult who is versatile and resourceful, always using their skills to solve problems.

What's more?

We see executive function as a mental process that occurs in the brain and is responsible for high-level thinking, decision-making, and emotional regulation. Skills related to executive functioning let us manage emotional responses and sustain our attention on a specific task. Also, executive function is strongly tied to planning, motivation, and goal setting. The parts of our brains responsible for these processes are not done developing by the time of our adolescence.

How is the adolescent brain changing?

Next, you probably need to know that your brain is not stagnant; it changes. Research has found that while some brain volume reaches adult levels through puberty, it is still maturing and becoming more effective until your mid-20s, especially when it comes to working memory and attentional skills that come with your capacity to make decisions. The continuously developing prefrontal cortex and improved responses in parts of the brain are responsible for emotional responses. Therefore, it is sufficient to say that many of these changes that the teenage brain went through may contribute to reward-seeking and risk-taking habits.

Diving deep into the 7 executive functions

1. Inhibitory Control

Let's start with inhibitory control because it plays a significant role in all functions. It regards your ability to stop doing what you shouldn't be doing at a specific time and place. As you grow up, you should rely on your parents to tell you what you shouldn't do at that moment. Have you wondered why, at a birthday party, all the teens there know when to settle down and eat, but only one person among them will still be bouncing or dancing, refusing to transit? I can relate personally. This happens because the teen has poor inhibitory control. Such a person does not always notice or respond to those changes that are expected to occur at a time. You may see such persons interrupting, yelling, or excusing themselves from the class even while there is a teacher present.

2. Self-monitoring

This concerns your awareness of how your actions or behaviors affect another person. As you can imagine, this is a crucial social skill. So, teens with self-awareness struggle socially because they don't understand what easily annoys or antagonizes other people.

3. Cognitive Flexibility

This can also be referred to as shift. It refers to your ability to move or switch from one situation to another. You can change your schedule easily or have the ability to alternate between two tasks. Teens who struggle with shifting are often poor problem-solvers. For example, a child might be expected to listen to the teacher, copy what is written on the board, and ask questions for clarification. This requires a lot of flexibility, which of course, has to do with teaching you to prioritize the most important information.

4. Emotional control

This is your ability to regulate emotions peculiar to a particular place and time. When a teen has poor emotional control, they usually have frequent tantrums or over-reaction that don't match the problem's size.

Working memory

In an academic setting, teens with poor working memory often forget the task they have at hand or get confused about complex situations. This is a small amount of mental ability to hold vital information in your mind to accomplish a task. It is vital for multi-step direction and to sustain your attention for a particular time.

5. Organization

This is about your ability to track your belongings and materials. For example, if you are given a book assignment in school and you get home but can't find the book, you likely have poor organizational skills. At home, such an issue will result in messy play spaces and the loss of many items.

6. Planning

This is your ability to think ahead, your ability to manage future activities and demands. This skill is important for setting goals and devising steps needed to accomplish them.

If you have poor planning strategies, you will struggle with time management. You may start a project right before it is meant to be submitted, simply because you don't realize the required planning strategies.

How are executive functioning and daily living skills related?

Most of your daily skills involve executive functioning behaviors. For you, learning daily living skills begins with primary needs. These are habits that help meet our basic survival needs. They include dressing, drinking water, safety, and household tasks such as cleaning and washing. All of these are covered under your primary needs.

Some of these primary needs are captured below:

Planning: This is your weekly schedule, such as school assignments, listing what you need for grocery shopping, and what you already have.

Organization: This involves organizational skills such as house chores, tidying up, washing, folding laundry, and organizing your belongings.

Time management: This involves teaching yourself how to manage time. It comes from teaching yourself morning and bedtime routines and encouraging yourself to finish any task you start at a defined time.

Flexibility: This involves developing flexible skills to change your daily routines.

Working memory and problem-solving: Building your working memory as a teenager comes by teaching yourself or being open to simple teaching on personal safety and basic community rules. You can help yourself rely on your knowledge of maneuvering problem-solving situations in your community.

Emotional and Impulse Control: This involves helping yourself learn how to control your impulses and emotions, especially regarding food choices.

Secondary Needs

Apart from the development that occurs as per your basic daily living skills, there are some secondary needs we also need to consider. As your primary daily living skills improve, you also develop the skills to meet your secondary needs. These are things like transportation (using public buses, driving, reading and interpreting road signs, and navigating maps), personal finance skills (savings, budget management, and basic investment, and career planning (goal setting, vocational training, and job search). Below are the areas you need to build your skills to meet your secondary needs as a teenager;

Working memory: This has to do with seeking help, perhaps from your parents, to know how to apply your community knowledge to get things around you. Things like navigating personal finances and using public transportation.

Time management: Learning to adjust to transportation schedules and budgeting more than enough time to travel to numerous places on a schedule. You need to enhance your capacity to keep to time when hanging out for anything.

Planning involves deciding which way to go among many options to get you from one point to another.

Self-monitoring: coming up with and sticking to a budget to reach a savings goal and develop and set goals for career and personal life.

Attentional control: This is also another vital area you need to develop as it entails building your attentional control, which has to do with using a bike, driving a car, or navigating through pedestrian lanes in a local environment.

Task Initiation: This has to do with teaching yourself to follow more complex routines and work through each step leading to your goal that may take longer to achieve. This category includes saving for a high-ticket item, applying to university, and getting your first job. All this needs proper planning and, thus, your ability to use your brain to initiate something.

Goal setting, planning, and task monitoring

Here, I would like to talk about self-regulation. It is vital for any goal-driven activity. Identifying planning and goals, monitoring progress, and shifting behavior are vital skills to practice.

How did this start?

Focus your mind on the planning process.

This has to do with identifying something specific that they want to do. Essentially, your goals are meaningful to you and not established by others. For some teens, planning a high school application may be self-motivating, but for others, planning a social event may feel more important. You need to focus your mind on the planning process.

I know you may not know how to do this, but I don't think you need to start big. You should start with something simple and achievable, like planning to save money to buy something small.

Have plans for steps to reach your goals

You should identify your long and short-term goals and reflect on what to do to achieve them. For example, if you want your team to win the sports championship, what skills do they need to learn? How might they practice them? Identify some challenges that might arise, and encourage you to plan.

Discussing large social issues

Domestic violence, homelessness, or bullying can be overwhelming and appealing for teens like you. So, you need to identify concrete actions that you do and have a discussion about social issues is the way through. VolunteerMatch.org and DoSomething.org.

Monitor your behavior

You must decide what you've planned and whether they are playing out. You can start by asking yourself, "Is this what I planned? If not, why am I doing it? Has something changed?" When you monitor this method, it can help you identify counter-productive and impulsive actions. It will also help you stay focused and be conscious of your control.

Tools for self-monitoring

I have been talking about how to do self-monitoring. I think it is better if I give you the tools to help you improve this.

Self-talk

This is a powerful tool you can deploy to bring your thoughts and actions into consciousness. Thoughts are not always aligned; they always scatter. Sometimes, it becomes difficult for you to grab one and implement it. With self-talk, you can periodically pause for a mental play-by-play narration of what's going around you. When occasions arise that generate strong negative feelings or emotions of failure, self-talk can help you identify impending thinking and behavior patterns.

So, how do you go about it?

1. Encourage self-talk that centers on growth.

You should learn to recognize that negative experiences can teach you lessons and should never be interpreted as a final judgment of your abilities.

For instance, when your team performs poorly in a debate competition, self-talk helps you or any other team members to consider when they miss it and what you or they might do to improve next time. That is the best way to go rather than deciding that your team lacks the skills to succeed.

2. Understanding the motivation that comes from others

Knowing the motivations of others when they offer them can be daunting, especially when perspectives drive people. So, you identify the rationale behind other people's motivations and then consider alternatives. "Why do you think she bumped into you? Can you think of another explanation?" Teens not used to this pattern may need to structure the process.

3. Writing a personal journal

Another way to foster self-reflection is to explore ideas, feelings, decisions, and beliefs. You can approach journaling in many ways, but all encourage self-planning, reflection, and awareness.

4. Be mindful of interruptions.

Doing many things simultaneously may feel good, but there is strong evidence that it consumes your energy, shifts your attention, and distracts you. Multitasking will also impede your performance. If you discover two tasks are competing for attention simultaneously, you should discuss how to prioritize them. This will help you attend to them in sequence. In summary, you must know that adolescence is not experiencing physical growth. You are also growing mentally. Your mental growth is as important as your physical growth because you need it to function effectively in your daily tasks, even as you become an adult. Prepare your mind and accommodate these changes as soon as possible so you can fully prepare for life's expectations.

Key Takeaways

- Adolescence is a phase that brings about different expectations and responsibilities across all spheres of your life as a teenager.

- Executive function, a mental process in the brain, is responsible for high-level thinking, decision-making, and emotional regulation.

- Research shows that while your total brain volume reaches adult levels by puberty, it will still mature and become more effective until you are in your mid-20s.

- Self-talk is a powerful tool you can deploy to bring your thoughts and actions into consciousness.

Chapter 3: Identifying and Assessing Executive Functioning Deficits

As a teen, your executive functioning skills play a big role in your daily life. They help you plan, organize, complete tasks and manage your emotions and impulses. These skills are important for your success in school, relationships, and other areas of your life. But what happens when you struggle with these skills? It could mean that you're experiencing executive function deficits that can cause organization, time management difficulties, and more. Don't worry; there are ways to identify and assess these challenges. In this chapter, we'll take a closer look at the signs and symptoms of executive function deficits in teens and explore the tools and assessments that can help you understand your challenges better.

Signs and symptoms of executive functioning deficits in teens

You know how important executive functioning is for success in many areas of life. But did you know that some people struggle with these skills? That's where executive functioning deficits come in. In this section, we'll dive into the common challenges you may face if you have these deficits, such as difficulties with organization, planning, and managing your time. By understanding these signs and symptoms, you can better understand your strengths and weaknesses in these areas and get the support you need to develop your skills.

Difficulty with planning and organization

So, have you ever found yourself struggling to keep track of your schedule or tasks for the day? Maybe you forget about upcoming deadlines or appointments or have trouble finding the best way to approach a project. These are all signs that you might have difficulty with planning and organization, a common symptom of executive functioning deficits.

It is frustrating when you want to get things done and you just can't seem to get organized. It can also make school or work more challenging because you cannot effectively complete assignments or meet deadlines.

Inability to prioritize tasks or set goals

The inability to prioritize tasks or set goals is another common symptom of teen executive function deficits. If you struggle with prioritizing tasks, you may be overwhelmed by multiple responsibilities and unsure where to start. This can lead to feeling stressed and frustrated, and it can be difficult to accomplish what you need to do.

Setting and achieving goals can also be challenging when you have executive function deficits. You may struggle to identify what you want to accomplish or have trouble creating a plan to reach your goals. This can make it difficult to stay motivated and progress toward your aspirations.

Impulsiveness and poor decision making

Many teens face two common symptoms of executive function deficits: impulsiveness and poor decision-making. When you struggle with impulsiveness, you may act without considering the consequences, leading you to make decisions or engage in behaviors you later regret. This can be seen in making impulsive purchases, saying things without thinking them through or engaging in risky behaviors.

Poor decision-making is another symptom that can make it difficult to weigh the pros and cons of different options and make a thoughtful, well-informed choice. This can result in struggling to choose between different options, making decisions based on immediate desires or impulses, or having trouble understanding the consequences of your choices. These symptoms can significantly impact your daily life, making it difficult to achieve your goals and succeed in school, work, and relationships. However, you can overcome these challenges and improve your executive functioning skills with the right support and resources. So, don't lose hope and keep pushing forward.

Poor time management skills

As a teen, when you struggle with managing your time effectively, you may find that you are often late to appointments or events. This can lead to difficulty forming and maintaining relationships and decreased trust from those around you. This is a common symptom of executive function deficits in teens and can affect your daily life.

Additionally, poor time management can lead to stress and anxiety as you try to balance schoolwork, extracurricular activities, and social time. You may often feel overwhelmed or find it difficult to complete tasks on time, resulting in lower grades or performance in school or other activities.

Finally, poor time management skills can also affect your future. If you struggle to meet deadlines, you may miss out on opportunities for internships, jobs, or scholarships. This can limit your options and opportunities in the long run.

Struggles with initiating tasks or following through with projects

Struggles with initiating tasks or following through with projects are also common symptoms of executive function deficits in teens. When you struggle with initiating tasks, you may have trouble getting started on important projects or assignments, even when you know they need to be done. This can lead to procrastination, making it difficult to meet deadlines and achieve your goals.

Following through with projects can also be challenging when you have executive function deficits. You may start a task with good intentions but then find yourself getting distracted or losing focus. This can result in incomplete projects, unfinished assignments, and frustration.

Challenges adapting to changes in routine or environment

This is another common symptom of executive function deficits in teens. When you struggle to adapt to changes in routine or environment, it can feel like the world is always shifting beneath your feet.

You may find it difficult to switch gears from one task to another or have trouble adjusting to new environments or situations. This can lead to you feeling anxious, overwhelmed, or stressed, especially in new or unfamiliar situations. For example, if you're used to studying in a quiet, familiar environment, you may struggle to adjust to taking a test in a noisy classroom. Or, if you're used to a set routine, you may struggle to adapt to a schedule change or unexpected event.

These difficulties can also impact your relationships, as those around you may become frustrated with your inability to adjust to changes or respond to new situations. Additionally, they can limit your ability to succeed in school, work, or other areas of your life, as you may struggle to perform well in new or unfamiliar situations.

Poor working memory, leading to difficulties retaining information

Working memory is the ability to retain and manipulate information in your mind for a short time. When you struggle with working memory, it can be difficult to remember what you just heard, read, or saw. This can make it challenging to complete tasks that require you to hold onto information and use it in real-time, such as taking notes in class or following multi-step instructions.

You may find that you forget important details, struggle to recall information you learned in the past, or have trouble following conversations or lectures. In addition, poor working memory can make it difficult to retain information over time. This can affect your school performance and your ability to learn and retain information in other areas of your life.

Struggles with regulating emotions and controlling impulses

Struggling with regulating emotions and controlling impulses can be incredibly frustrating and have a major impact on your life. For example, when you're struggling to regulate your emotions, it may feel like you're on an emotional rollercoaster. One moment, you might feel fine, but the next, something sets you off, and you're overwhelmed with intense feelings. This can lead to feeling irritable or easily upset and make it difficult to handle stress or relationships with others.

When it comes to controlling impulses, the lack of control can make it difficult to plan for the future and make decisions that are best for you in the long run. For example, you might make an impulsive purchase that you later regret or act impulsively in a social situation and say or do something that damages a relationship.

These difficulties can also impact your ability to succeed in school, work, or other areas of your life, as impulsiveness can get in the way of making well-thought-out decisions and achieving your goals.

Difficulty with multitasking and managing multiple demands.

This is another common symptom of executive function deficits in teens. When you struggle with multitasking, it can feel like too many things are going on at once, and you don't know where to begin. This can lead to feeling overwhelmed, stressed, and confused, making it difficult to stay on top of all your responsibilities. Managing multiple demands, such as schoolwork, extracurricular activities, and social commitments, can be especially challenging. You may find that you're constantly switching between tasks and having trouble focusing on any one thing for a very long time. This can make it difficult to complete tasks to the best of your ability, resulting in mistakes or a lower quality of work. Difficulty with multitasking and managing multiple demands can be challenging, but with adequate strategies, you can learn to manage your time and responsibilities better.

The tools and assessments that can identify and measure a teen's executive functioning skills

Understanding your executive functioning skills is important for your personal and academic growth as a teenager. Understanding your executive functioning skills can help you work towards developing strategies for success and reaching your full potential. Various tools and assessments can help you determine your strengths and areas of improvement in these skills. This section will look into the different types of assessments used to identify and measure executive functioning skills.

Behavioral rating scales

So, when it comes to behavioral rating scales, you might have a parent, teacher, or other caregiver fill out a questionnaire about your executive functioning skills.

This questionnaire will likely ask questions about different areas of executive functioning, such as how well you manage your time, regulate your emotions, and control your impulses. For example, they might ask questions like:

- "Does the teen have difficulty managing their time effectively?"

- "Does the teen struggle with regulating their emotions when faced with stress or frustration?"

- "Does the teen act impulsively or make decisions without thinking them through?"

By asking these questions and collecting information from someone who interacts with you regularly, the questionnaire can provide valuable insights into your strengths and challenges regarding executive functioning.

So, a behavioral rating scale might be a good place to start if you're a teen looking to better understand your executive functioning skills.

Neuropsychological assessments

Neuropsychological assessments are another tool that can be used to identify and measure executive functioning skills in teens.

If you undergo a neuropsychological assessment, you'll likely meet with a licensed psychologist who will administer a series of tests to assess your cognitive and emotional abilities, including your executive functioning skills. These tests can be paper-and-pencil, computer-based, or a combination of both.

The tests you'll take during a neuropsychological assessment will be designed to evaluate different aspects of executive functioning, such as your attention, memory, problem-solving skills, and ability to plan and organize. The psychologist will use the results from these tests to better understand your executive functioning skills and identify any areas where you may need additional support.

Self-report questionnaires

Self-reported questionnaires are another tool that can be used to assess executive functioning skills in teens. With this type of assessment, you'll be asked to complete a questionnaire that assesses your executive functioning skills. This questionnaire might ask you how well you manage your time, regulate your emotions, control your impulses, and perform other tasks requiring executive functioning skills. For example, you might be asked questions like:

- "How often do you forget to complete tasks or follow through on your plans?"

- "Do you struggle to control your emotions when stressed or frustrated?"

- "Do you make impulsive decisions or act without thinking them through?"

By completing this questionnaire, you'll have the opportunity to reflect on your executive functioning skills and provide valuable insights into your strengths and challenges.

Direct observations

Direct observations are another way to assess executive functioning skills in teens. With direct observations, someone will observe you in real-life situations and take notes on your behavior and performance in areas such as time management, emotional control, and impulse control. This could involve observing you in a school or work setting or even in your daily life outside those settings. For example, they might observe the following:

- How you regulate your emotions in stressful or challenging situations

- How well you control your impulses and make thoughtful decisions

By observing you in real-life situations, the observer can better understand your executive functioning skills and identify any areas where you may need additional support.

Computerized assessments

Another tool used to assess executive functioning skills is computerized assessments. With computerized assessments, you'll use a computer program to complete tasks that measure specific aspects of your executive functioning, such as your working memory, attention, and impulsivity. These tasks might involve things like:

- Remembering and repeating sequences of numbers

- Respond quickly to visual or auditory stimuli

- Making decisions and solving problems under time pressure

By completing these tasks, the computer program can generate a report that provides insight into your executive functioning skills and identifies any areas where you may need additional support.

In conclusion, executive functioning skills are crucial in our daily lives. For teens who struggle with executive functioning, it can lead to difficulties with organization, time management, and other challenges. Identifying and assessing functioning executive deficits is the first step in supporting teens in developing these skills and reaching their full potential. You can better understand executive functioning skills and provide targeted support where needed through behavioral rating scales, neuropsychological assessments, self-report questionnaires, direct observations, and computerized assessments.

Key Takeaways

- Impulsiveness and poor decision-making are two common symptoms of executive function deficits that many teens face

- Poor time management can lead to stress and anxiety as you try to balance schoolwork, extracurricular activities, and social time

- If you're a teen looking to understand your executive functioning skills better, a behavioral rating scale might be a good place to start

Chapter 4: Strategies for Improving Executive Functioning

In the previous chapter, you learned about the challenges facing teens with executive functioning deficits. If you have been facing such challenges, you're not alone. Many teens face similar challenges when it comes to executive functioning. But don't worry; there is good news! Many strategies and interventions can help improve your executive functioning and make it easier for you to handle daily challenges.

In this chapter, we'll dive into these strategies and explore the various activities and exercises you can do to improve each component of executive functioning, including self-control, mental flexibility, working memory, and more. So, get ready to take control of your brain and improve your executive functioning skills.

Cognitive-behavioral therapy

Cognitive-behavioral therapy (CBT) is a type of therapy that can be incredibly helpful for improving executive functioning. This therapy focuses on changing negative patterns of thinking and behavior that make it difficult for you to reach your goals. By working with a therapist, you'll learn how to identify and replace negative patterns with positive, helpful ones.

Here's how it works: During a typical CBT session, you'll sit down with your therapist and talk about your struggles. Maybe you have difficulty staying focused in class, or you're feeling overwhelmed and disorganized. Whatever it is, your therapist will help you understand why these things are happening and what you can do to change them.

For example, let's say you're having trouble staying focused in class. Your therapist might help you figure out what's causing the distractions, such as thoughts about what's going on in your personal life or a lack of sleep. Then, you'll work together to develop strategies for staying focused, like taking breaks every hour to stretch and refocus your attention or breaking down big tasks into smaller, more manageable chunks.

CBT is a powerful tool for improving executive functioning because it helps you understand the connection between your thoughts, emotions, and behavior. By learning how to control these three things, you'll have more control over your life and be able to achieve your goals more effectively.

So, if you're seeking to boost your executive functioning and take control of your life, consider giving CBT a try.

Mindfulness

Mindfulness is a practice that can help you improve your executive functioning by reducing stress and increasing focus. The basic idea of mindfulness is to pay attention to the present moment without judgment.

Think about it: it can be hard to stay focused and organized when you're feeling stressed or overwhelmed. That's because your mind is racing, thinking about the future or past. But when you practice mindfulness, you learn to let go of those distractions and focus on the present.

One way to get started with mindfulness is through meditation. Simply locate a peaceful area to sit or lie down, close your eyes, and concentrate on your breathing. If your mind deviates, simply bring your attention to your breathing. Over time, you'll find that you're able to stay focused for longer and longer periods.

Mindfulness can also be practiced in your daily life. You can try mindful breathing throughout the day or even incorporate mindfulness into your hobby or exercise routine. For example, if you love to draw, try focusing all your attention on the pencil in your hand and how it feels against the paper.

The more you practice mindfulness, the easier it will be to stay focused and organized. Plus, you'll feel less stressed and more relaxed, which is great for your overall well-being.

So, give mindfulness a try if you're looking for a simple, effective way to boost your executive functioning.

Physical exercise

Physical exercise is another simple yet powerful way to improve executive functioning. When you perform physical activities, your body releases endorphins, which are feel-good chemicals that boost your mood and reduce stress. But that's not all! Exercise can also help you improve your focus, memory, and problem-solving skills.

One good thing about exercise is that you have so many options to choose from. Maybe you love to run, play basketball, or dance. Or maybe you prefer more low-impact exercises like yoga or swimming. Make sure you enjoy whatever you choose so you can stick to it more easily.

A great way to get started is by exercising for 20-30 minutes daily, 3-4 times a week. This could be a short walk, a yoga class, or a quick basketball game with friends. The key is to find something you love and make it a routine.

As you get into the habit of exercising, you'll start to see improvements in your focus, memory, and problem-solving skills. Plus, you'll have more energy and feel better about yourself, which is great for your overall well-being.

So, if you're looking for a fun and effective way to boost your executive functioning, try adding physical exercise to your routine. You'll be amazed at the results.

Sleep hygiene

Sleep is also important for improving executive functioning. When you get enough quality sleep, you'll be better able to focus, remember things, and solve problems. On the other hand, when you don't get enough sleep, you'll feel tired, irritable, and have a hard time staying focused.

To ensure you get the best sleep possible, try to develop good sleep hygiene habits. This means creating a bedtime routine that helps you wind down before sleep and creating a comfortable sleep environment. For example, you might try reading a book, meditating, or doing a relaxing activity before bed. You could also try to make your room as dark and quiet as possible and keep the temperature cool.

If you cultivate appropriate sleep hygiene habits, you will be able to fall asleep faster, sleep through the entirety of the night, and wake up feeling rejuvenated and ready to face the day ahead. Also, avoid using electronic devices such as your phone, tablet, or computer before bed because the blue light they create can disrupt sleep. Consider using a classic alarm clock rather than your phone to further eliminate distractions.

Prioritize sleep and develop good sleep hygiene habits if you want to improve your executive functioning. Your brain will thank you.

Specific activities and exercises for developing each component of executive functioning.

Self-control (inhibitory)

Self-control is an important part of executive functioning. Unfortunately, lots of teenagers struggle with self-control. I have listed some ways to improve the inhibitory component of executive functioning.

Delaying gratification

Delaying gratification exercises play a crucial role in developing the self-control or inhibitory component of executive functioning. This component is about controlling your impulses, thoughts, and actions, especially in challenging situations. It could be as simple as waiting to eat that piece of candy until after you finish your homework or saving your allowance to buy a bigger toy later on.

You strengthen your inhibitory control when you practice delaying gratification by resisting immediate temptations and distractions. This can help you stay focused on the task at hand, avoid impulsive decisions, and make better choices in the long run. It's like building muscle; the more you practice, the stronger it becomes.

By engaging in these exercises, you are actively working on improving your self-control, which is an important aspect of executive functioning.

Impulse control activities

Impulse control activities are another great way to develop the inhibitory component of executive functioning. One fun example is playing a self-control game, which specifically tests and improves your ability to resist temptations and distractions.

Here's how it works: imagine you have a jar of candy in front of you, and the goal is to resist eating any of it until a set amount of time has passed. Sounds simple, right? But as time passes, the temptation to eat the candy will grow, testing your impulse control.

Playing games like this can help you learn to manage your impulses, reduce distractions, and improve your ability to focus on the task. It's also a great way to have fun while developing important life skills! So why not give it a try? You might be surprised at how challenging it can be, but with practice, you'll get better and better at it.

Mental (cognitive) flexibility

Wondering how to improve your mental flexibility? In this section, you will learn some practices that can help you develop your cognitive flexibility.

Brain-training exercises

Brain-training exercises, such as those that require switching between tasks, can help you practice this skill and improve your mental flexibility over time.

For example, you could try playing a game requiring you to switch between different tasks, such as matching objects or solving puzzles. Another option is to set a timer and switch between different activities, like writing, reading, and solving math problems, every time the timer goes off.

Regularly engaging in brain-training exercises can improve your mental flexibility, making it easier to handle life's challenges and be more productive in your daily tasks. These types of exercises can be fun and challenging, and they'll help you practice quickly adjusting to new information and changing demands. Give it a try.

Problem-solving games that involve finding multiple solutions to a single problem

Another great way to develop mental (cognitive) flexibility is by playing problem-solving games that involve finding multiple solutions to a problem.

These games require you to think creatively and come up with different solutions to a problem, which can help you practice generating multiple ideas and considering different perspectives. This exercise helps improve cognitive flexibility by challenging you to be open-minded and flexible in your thinking.

For example, you could try a game where you can escape a room by finding clues and solving puzzles. Another option is a strategy game where you must find multiple ways to achieve a goal. These types of games will help you develop your mental flexibility, problem-solving skills, and overall creativity.

Cognitive tasks that challenge your ability to adjust to new information or changes in rules

Another effective way to develop mental (cognitive) flexibility is by engaging in cognitive tasks that challenge your ability to adjust to new information or changes in rules. This exercise helps to improve cognitive flexibility by requiring you to adapt to new information or changes in rules, which can be a valuable skill in real-life situations.

For example, you could try playing a game that involves changing rules, like a card game where the rules keep changing every round. Another option is a task that requires you to quickly adjust to new information, like a memory game where the cards are constantly changing. These activities will help you develop mental flexibility, adaptability, and overall cognitive skills.

Working Memory

Working memory is another important component of executive functioning. Here are some activities tailored to help you develop your working memory:

Memory improvement techniques, such as visualization and chunking

One effective way to improve working memory is using memory improvement techniques, such as visualization and chunking.

Visualization involves creating mental images of information to help you remember it better. For example, if you're trying to remember a list of grocery items, you can imagine each item in your mind and visualize yourself placing them in your shopping cart.

Chunking involves breaking information down into smaller, more manageable pieces. For example, instead of trying to remember a long phone number, you can chunk it into smaller groups of numbers, such as (555) 123-4567. This makes it easier to process and recall information.

So, if you want to improve your working memory, try using visualization and chunking techniques. They can help you process and recall information more effectively, improving your performance in school and everyday life.

Working memory exercises, such as complex arithmetic problems or keeping track of multiple items

Another great way to develop working memory is through working memory exercises, such as complex arithmetic problems or keeping track of multiple items.

Working memory exercises can help improve your ability to hold information in your mind, which is important for many daily tasks, like following instructions, solving problems, and making decisions.

For example, you could try solving complex arithmetic problems like mental math exercises to improve your working memory. You can also try keeping track of multiple items, like remembering a list of grocery items, while shopping for other items in the store.

Mental exercises that challenge your ability to keep information in your mind and manipulate it

Another great way to develop working memory is through mental exercises that challenge your ability to keep and manipulate information in your mind.

These exercises can help improve your ability to hold and manipulate information, which is important for daily tasks like following instructions, solving problems, and making decisions.

For example, you could try mentally rearranging a set of numbers or letters, like putting the letters "H-O-R-S-E" in alphabetical order. Or, you could try remembering a list of words and then recall them in a different order.

Games that challenge your working memory capacity, such as memory matching games.

Memory matching games, for instance, are a fun and engaging way to improve your working memory. In these games, you must match pairs of items by recalling their locations, often under time pressure. This requires you to use your working memory to keep track of multiple pieces of information and manipulate it as needed.

Let's say you're playing a memory-matching game where you have to match pairs of cards with different shapes and colors. To play, you must flip over two cards simultaneously, trying to find a match. When you find a match, you keep the cards and get points. If you don't find a match, you must remember where the cards are so you can try to match them later.

As you play the game, you'll be using your working memory to keep track of the different shapes and colors you've already seen and the location of each card. By regularly playing memory-matching games, you'll be strengthening your working memory.

In conclusion, developing your executive functioning skills can profoundly impact your daily life. Whether it's through mindfulness practices, physical exercise, or targeted activities and exercises, there are many strategies you can use to improve each component of your executive functioning. Remember, these skills take time and practice to develop, but the more you invest in them, the more you'll see positive results.

Key Takeaways

- Cognitive-behavioral therapy (CBT) is a type of therapy that can be incredibly helpful for improving executive functioning.

- When you practice delaying gratification, you are strengthening your inhibitory control by resisting immediate temptations and distractions.

- Visualization and chunking techniques can help you process and recall information more effectively.

- Physical exercise is a simple yet powerful way to improve executive functioning.

Chapter 5: Applying Executive Functioning Skills

"Executive functioning is not about knowing things. It's about using what you know for effective performance in life-for social, occupational, and educational effectiveness".

When you apply your executive functioning skills, you become useful for yourself and society. By practicing your executive functioning skills daily, you will perform better in every area of your life, like your social life, career, academic situation, time management, and situational awareness. These skills will form a good attitude, allowing you to choose the best for yourself. Your peer group will reckon with you and learn from you, especially those without executive functioning skills. Research reveals that teenagers with improved executive functioning skills usually perform better academically. A meta-analysis of six studies discovered that a child's executive functioning skills in kindergarten predict their mathematics and reading achievement in high school and later. Recent studies reveal that executive functioning skills are more significant to teenagers' success than academic performance and intelligence. When you get to college, these skills will help you manage your time judiciously, finish your assignments quickly, organize social obligations, and become athletes. Hence, this chapter will focus on how improved executive functioning skills can be applied in different areas of your life, as examples of how improved executive functioning skills can benefit you in academics, social interactions, and time management. Additionally, it will include case studies and real-life examples of teens who have successfully improved their executive functioning skills and how they have positively impacted their lives.

The daily application of executive skills

Your executive functioning skills are significant throughout your lifetime. The cognitive processes support you in regulating and directing your behavior to achieve your goals. You and your environment will experience lifelong benefits if you apply your executive functioning skills. Also, know that applying these skills requires commitment and discipline. With the two attributes, you will become better.

Below are a few examples of executive functioning skills application:

Build a schedule or planner

One of the best ways to apply your improved executive functioning skills is to create a good system to manage your assignments. To achieve this, you can use planning and organizational skills. Also, you can use color coding to prioritize your significant tasks.

Studying

Studying includes perusing a book, writing, and solving mathematical questions. The materials might look boring or difficult, but be persistent in your effort to complete the tasks. All you need to do while studying is pay critical attention.

Another way of applying your improved executive functioning skills is by developing a quiet area where you can personally study without distraction. If unnecessary, let the environment be free of electronic devices, including your smartphone. Consider filling the environment with essential educational materials to minimize interruption or distraction. A quiet environment encourages active learning. By creating a silent place for your studies, you will actively pay attention and focus on what you are reading, and your memory will retain vital information.

Examine your understanding

Try to examine your academic performance or abilities in each subject. Know your weaknesses and strengths in each subject. Identify the ones you have self-confidence in and those you need to build self-confidence in. Through that, you are implementing the two components of executive function: self-evaluation and self-reflection.

Engage in what you love most

Everyone has one activity they love to do. Do not neglect activities you are passionate about; always engage in them. Engaging in your hobbies will help you apply your executive functioning skills, such as planning, time management, and self-directed learning. Try to plan the time you will start the activities and the time that you will stop. Also, know the kind of hobbies you want to engage in. For instance, you can schedule an hour or more to play musical instruments or video games. Ensure that you stick to the schedule for the activity. And if you decide to engage in more than one activity, schedule the time you will spend on each activity.

Completing a project

A project might be building a model or planning a social event. You may even be involved in a group project where individuals involved will think of the ideas and plan the necessary resources. Others might not even have executive functioning skills like planning and time management. You have to coordinate them by planning how to achieve the project before the deadline. And if there's any challenge, you must be flexible enough to adapt.

Littering

The force to throw a tin, bottle, wrapper, or paper on the floor as soon as you have exhausted the content inside it is often strong, especially if your hands are full of other things. Instead of littering your environment, you can control the impulse by putting the trash in your bag or pocket until you see a trash can to dispose of the items. Every individual has the power to control themselves, and you are no different.

Control yourself by keeping your room and environment clean.

Multitasking

Multitasking occurs when you are handling more than one task at once. Examples of multitasking include listening to your teacher's explanation while making notes, conversing with your friends while surfing the internet, watching your favorite TV program while eating, performing your routine, and at the same time preparing for the next thing, etc.

Cleaning your wardrobes

Cleaning your wardrobe frequently is an essential task that requires organizational skills. It would help if you organized your clothes in your wardrobe according to occasion, season, and color. You can also organize your books on your shelf according to genre and size. You are applying your executive functioning skills by organizing your personal belongings to fit your shelf, wardrobe, or furniture for convenience.

Playing a game

Playing a game entails executing many different tasks, which include thinking or recalling a game, creating the required number of players, dividing the players, and clarifying the rules. Planning the game, following the rules, and ensuring every player gets a fair turn are all tasks you can perform because of your executive functioning skills.

Going to the theater

Going to the theater requires you to maintain attention throughout the movie or show to comprehend and enjoy the story. It also entails regulating your feelings about the story and expressing them softly or after the movie so as not to disturb others.

Communicating

Effective communication requires many skills. While conversing with other people, you must pay active attention and actively listen to them. If you disagree with their opinions, respect their views and express your dissent appropriately. However, it would help if you also displayed conversation-appropriate emotions and gestures like nodding, smiling gently, and looking at the other conversation participant in the eye to indicate you are active with them. It would be advised that you don't start laughing at any serious moments during the conversation.

Eating

Some people have the urge to avoid all vegetables when eating. Vegetables are a key part of a balanced diet and should not be ignored. By resisting the urge to leave your vegetables, you are controlling an unhealthy impulse, which is one of the executive functioning skills.

How the examples of executive functioning skills can benefit you:

Suppose executive functioning skills can be the cognitive processes that help you regulate and direct your behavior to achieve your goals. In that case, the skills will greatly impact every area of your life, from your academics to how you manage your time. Below are the benefits of executive functioning skills for you:

Time management

Time management plays a crucial role in your productivity. Intelligent children without good time management will always have difficulty displaying what they know effectively. To achieve academic success, you must prioritize your activities. For instance, if you have many tasks on a deadline, consider first attending to the ones you know you can do faster and attending to the rest when you are done.

With time management, you will get to school on time; you won't miss any appointments or get there late, and you will get to social events at the correct time.

With time management, you will be structured in your daily activities. For instance, you won't be watching TV while you should be studying. You will have allocated different moments in the day to all your activities. Sticking to them will help you complete them at the right time.

Time management enables you to use your time judiciously to avoid regret afterward. You'll be able to avoid the feeling that you wasted your time doing something unproductive and failed to put enough time into doing something that will have a positive benefit on your life.

With time management, you will excel in study skills and maintain time to build your social life.

Academic Performance

Executive functioning skills have a great influence on your academic performance. Parts of the skills for school are planning and self-regulation. Focusing on what your teacher or coach is saying requires self-discipline. It also takes discipline for you to plan big projects. With executive functioning skills, you can manage increased workloads without outside input. You can also maintain the increasing demands at school, plan long-term assignments and carry out demanding tasks without giving up.

Social interaction

Social interaction is a mutual influence implemented by two or more people during social experiences. It often means face-to-face encounters in which people physically present with one another.

Circumnavigating social interactions entails many mental processes or executive functioning skills.

Executive functioning skills help you to adapt easily to a new environment.

With executive functioning skills, you can relate with other teenagers from different backgrounds without having issues with them.

Executive functioning skills enable you to know how to organize yourself in a social gathering. You talk when you ought to talk and listen actively when you ought to.

The skills allow you to face the crowd regardless of their numbers.

Teenagers with executive functioning skills know how to manage their time when they are given a chance to handle public speaking.

Case studies and real-life examples of teens who have successfully improved their executive functioning skills and how they have positively impacted their lives

Example 1

Jack was a bright, diligent, and talented teen who struggled with procrastination and organization, especially when writing and researching assignments. Because of the pandemic, he started his freshman first term from home. In January 2021, Jack's parents discovered 20 missing assignments in his school's database at the end of his second term in high school.

He told his mother he had enough time to do other things besides his assignments. He preferred watching Netflix to writing his assignments or studying. His parents tried to help him, but all effort was to no avail. His mother decided to reach out to an outsider who could help them.

His tutor discovered that Jack was striving with what other teens were struggling with, like task initiation, prioritization, organization, and time management.

Jack's tutor began to teach him executive functioning and put the executive functioning strategies into practice. His tutor met with him on Google Meet, where she engaged and also monitored his assignments and school work. After two months, Jack changed. His grades improved, and he took his working habits seriously.

Example 2

In April 2012, Jake discussed his academic issues with his friend. Jake wanted to fix the issue but did not know how to go about it. His friend asked him if he had a task routine; unfortunately, Jake did not. Jake explained to his friend that he got his assignments done after he had played outside. Jake's grades reflected the inconsistency of his non-strategic approach. He strived with his grades that year and got what he didn't expect.

During their conversation, Jake's friend deduced that Jake desired to do well, but he despised everything about school and would not stay with boring work. Jake said he preferred to play outside, which led to his lack of focus. Jake found it difficult to push through any challenges he encountered.

Jake was introduced to an executive function coach who could help him. His coach discovered that Jake was struggling with sustaining attention, task completion, and organization. With the help of his coach, who used executive functioning skills strategies for him, Jake was able to execute new strategies for test preparation, time management, and organization.

When Jake resumed school, he returned and placed his lunch box where it was supposed to be without any instruction from anyone. He also reflected more consistent effort in his schoolwork. He mapped out weekly activities without or with little support. His mother noticed him building and reaching a higher level of self-esteem and self-confidence. With executive functioning skills, Jake always looks forward to his new school year with high academic success. Implementation of executive functioning skills has positively impacted Jake's life. Jake eventually knew that a feeling of success was worth the quality time spent facing his challenges. He's excelling in all spheres of life now.

Key Takeaway

- Your executive functioning skills are significant throughout your lifetime

- The best time to engage in your hobbies is during your pastime to enjoy yourself accurately

- Parts of the skills for school are planning and self-regulation

Chapter 6: Executive Functioning Skills One-By-One

In the previous chapters, I discussed various components of executive functioning skills with you. By components, I mean techniques or strategies where executive functioning skills are applicable. However, I must take you through each skill, one after the other, to examine them and how they apply to you. We need to discuss them extensively to know how they relate to your everyday activities and how you can improve on them.

A.   Time management strategies:

Time management involves having a better understanding of time and making decisions to get tasks done on time. Time management is not like most other executive functioning skills because it is not a standalone skill. It involves estimating how long tasks will take, which one to attend to first, and allotting tasks between time. It involves using your time wisely, pacing yourself, and working to meet deadlines, especially if it is your schoolwork.

Examples of what strong time management skills may look like include:

• Prioritizing which homework or assignment to attend to first before picking up others

• Pacing yourself on a test or exam to ensure you get done on time

• Listing out your daily schedules to ensure you keep track of time and events

• Insert a task into sections to get it done by a specific deadline

Like the rest of the executive skills, the ability to manage your time can be strengthened or improved over time. Below are some ideas, techniques, or activities to help you achieve that.

• Make a list of all your assignments and go back to putting them in order of importance

• Create a checklist for a set of tasks or steps

- Estimate your time for different takes (You can even deploy a gaming strategy! How long do you think it would take to get this assignment done?)

- Leverage visual timer

- Leverage chimes to warn you when your time of transition is getting near. You can set it to 5 to 0 minutes.

- Maintain a regular and consistent daily schedule

- Put your schedules on the top of your desk in school and on the wall of your room

- Identify your distractions and tag them as 'time-eaters'

- Devise a way to move on when you get stuck

- Play time-based games (Don't forget to add a timer to the games you want to play. Scramble and Pictionary are very good time-based games)

- Break down large projects into smaller tasks

- Leverage time-management tools and apps, such as calendars and more

B. Planning and organization techniques:

As you've read many times in this book, planning, and organization involve developing a well-thought technique to handle a task even before starting. See planning as a game. You need to think critically before playing. This skill is needed when you are thinking about which materials to bring before leaving or have used a computer to list important upcoming dates. In every way, planning pays off! When you plan well, you save yourself valuable time and effort because you've got it right the first time.

Some examples of where accurate planning wins include:

•   Writing down your assignment as an agenda before the close of the class

•   Taking a few minutes to think about what could be done before taking any step

•   Having a proper time to plan game time, assignments, and chores so that activities don't overlap.

- Figuring out which college to attend and for what career.

- Losing or misplacing class assignment

- Having a messy desk

- Difficulty in transitioning from one class to another

- Fail or forget to bring necessary classroom materials, such as a pencil, or correct binder, to the classroom

Planning and organization are very important for you to succeed inside and outside your classroom. Below are some ideas, techniques, or activities to help you achieve that

- Have a to-do list before starting any assignment, especially the longer ones

- Use a calendar

- Use a rubric for large assignments

- Keep your daily objectives and schedules in view

- Always keep important dates in sight

- Practice SMART goals and ensure you follow through with them

- Leverage behavioral reflection pages to consider available choices.

- Use the free homework binder

- Talk about how you want to spend your day in the morning meetings.

- Use planning apps such as Trello, MyHomework, and Evernote

- Track tasks, such as creating a schedule, using a planner, and setting reminders

- Use every last 3 minutes of class to organize yourself

C. Goal-setting and decision-making skills

Goal-setting and decision-making skills are important parts of executive function skills that you should develop. This is about your ability to set achievable goals and work towards achieving them. If you ask me how best you can do this, I would advise you to go for SMART goals. What are SMART goals? SMART is an acronym for specific, measurable, achievable, realistic, and time-bound goals.

Some examples where goal-setting and decision-making skills are important are:

• Clearly state what your goals are (for instance, let's say you want to be the best student in your class, you then need to plan on attending class regularly, reading very and understanding very well, and attending to your homework, tests, and exams very well.)

• Mapping out strategies on how you will achieve those goals (plans are listed above). Have a reading timetable at home, and don't miss reading time.

In decision-making, you need to consider the pros and cons of your decision. For example, if you decide not to attend class regularly, there is a tendency that you may struggle to transition to the next class. You may need to consider your options by weighing them.

Doing that may also have to do with evaluating some potential outcomes.

Ask yourself;

•   What are the possible outcomes of what I am about to do?

•   Are there tangible reasons why I should take this step?

•   Are there other options I can explore besides what I have right now?

When you begin ruminating, many ideas will pop into your brain, and then you will leave to choose the options you want. But as I said, ensure you set a goal that is not achievable. The truth is that some goals are far beyond achievable. Ensure whatever you plan falls under the tenet of SMART goals so you can rest assured that you are not merely wishing or daydreaming.

D. Self-monitoring and self-evaluation

Are you good at stopping and reflecting on a particular move or step before you take it? Then you have a high sense of self-control and monitoring. Often, this involves thinking through a situation before taking a move. Of course, this can be challenging for you as you are in a stage where your mind is growing. But you start with real-life questions or scenarios such as, "What would I do in this particular situation?" "How do I react to this situation or deal with it?" If you can do this often before you take any step, you will become someone who doesn't act based on impulse alone. Other techniques you can deploy include learning to 'pause' or slow down when things are going very fast. This is when you need to pause and take a deep breath and do a self-task to check whether what you are doing is right or needed at that time.

Let me explain this in a social context. Let's say you meet a guy or lady that caught your attention. You like the person, but the person doesn't feel the same for you. But each day you see the person, you always want to force the energy, wanting to push the person to kiss or be romantic. You always want to get physical, even if the person does not feel the same way. You require self-control to allow things to flow naturally without forcing them.

Below are ideas you can deploy to do self-monitoring and evaluation.

• Having a checklist

• Have communication skills (where you input all your behaviors throughout the day)

• Have an Impulse control journal or frequency collection sheet

E. Problem-solving and critical thinking:

Knowing how to solve problems is one of the essential habits every teenager must have. This is important because as you grow, you will have to deal with many conflicts and face many options you must explore or develop strategies to overcome. Thus, this involves critical thinking – the ability to engage your mind when there is a problem and devise viable solutions. This also has to do with your ability to identify and analyze obstacles with the mind to proffer possible solutions. Teenagers who lack this skill might not be able to do well in any subject that involves calculations or critical thinking.

How to Develop Critical Thinking Skills

• Ask questions on areas you are not cleared within the class

• Don't believe you are always correct

• Think deeply

• Don't believe everything you are told

• Evaluate your schoolwork and assignments

• Practice active listening, especially when your teacher is teaching in class

• Build your foresight

• Question assumptions

• Do your research and accept only the fact

• Consider multiple views or perspectives

Under these skills, I will also discuss task initiation and attention because they are skills that address problems.

(A)   Task Initiation

This is due to your ability to start a project or task independently. This skill helps you get up and go even when you don't feel like it. This skill is difficult to figure out because it looks like you are just doing what you are supposed to, for example, waking up from bed and getting dressed up for school in the morning.

Examples of what this skill looks like are:

•   Starting your assignment immediately in class after the direction is given.

•   Cleaning your room when it needs to be done without being reminded

•   Starting a tough quiz or test, even when you are not confident you are going to score good grades.

You can develop this skill by imploring these ideas or strategies

•   Practice brain breaks when you have many tasks to do

•   Work with a partner on an assignment

•   Use a timer to get work done on time

- Keep a reminder card on your desk in school and inside your room at home

(B) Attention

This has to do with focusing or concentrating on a particular task. Besides focusing, this skill is also needed to refocus attention when the mind wanders off through distractions and fine-tune the focus needed to complete a task.

Below are strategies for gaining attention

- Always check in with yourself.

- Set a timer when you are doing any assignment

- Use the focus app

- Give yourself extra time to complete a task

- Avoid distractions around your room or in the classroom. In summary, each component of executive function is worth looking into, so you can identify the skills you don't have and those you need to improve as you become an adult. As you grow into adulthood, you must become intentional about building these skills because they are what you need to thrive. The fact is that life will throw a lot at you, that you need a strong dimension of these skills to stand.

Key Takeaways

- Knowing how to solve problems is one of the habits every teenager must have.
- Time management is about managing your time wisely, pacing yourself, and working to meet deadlines, especially if it has to do with your school work.
- Planning and organization involve developing a well-thought-out technique to handle a task before starting.

Chapter 7: Activities to Improve Executive Functioning

Executive functioning skills develop throughout childhood and adolescence and can be improved with practice and training. Having solid executive functioning skills can help you manage time, prioritize tasks, regulate emotions, and make responsible decisions.

In this chapter, we will explore different activities that can help improve your executive functioning, including mindfulness and meditation practices, physical exercise and movement, brain-stimulating games and puzzles, study skills and memory techniques, and social and emotional learning activities. By engaging in these activities, you can develop and strengthen your executive functioning skills, improving overall well-being and success in your personal and academic lives.

Mindfulness and meditation

Mindfulness and meditation have been around for thousands of years and have been shown to have many benefits for both physical and mental well-being. Mindfulness is the method of being present in the moment and paying full attention to your thoughts, feelings, and physical sensations without judgment. Meditation is a similar practice that involves focusing your mind and bringing awareness to the present moment.

There are many different techniques for practicing mindfulness and meditation, but they all aim to help you develop greater awareness and calmness. Some standard techniques include deep breathing exercises, guided meditations, and body scans. These practices can be done anywhere, at any time, and can be especially helpful for reducing stress and improving focus and attention.

Studies have shown that mindfulness and meditation can positively impact various physical and mental health issues, such as reducing symptoms of anxiety and depression, lowering blood pressure, and improving sleep. They can also help you develop greater self-awareness and compassion, improving relationships and overall life satisfaction.

Mindfulness and meditation are simple yet powerful tools that help you develop more significant focus, reduce stress, and improve your overall well-being.

Mindfulness and meditation have numerous benefits for you, especially when it comes to focusing, attention, and stress reduction. Here are some of the key benefits:

- **Improved Focus and Attention:** Mindfulness and meditation help train the brain to be more focused and attentive by encouraging individuals to pay attention to the present moment without distraction. This can lead to improved concentration, better memory, and a reduced risk of forgetfulness.

- **Stress Reduction:** Mindfulness and meditation effectively reduce stress and anxiety levels. By encouraging you to be present and focus on your thoughts and feelings without judgment, these practices help reduce feelings of stress and improve overall well-being.

- **Improved Mental Health:** Regular practice of mindfulness and meditation can help reduce symptoms of depression and anxiety and improve overall mental health. By learning to be more mindful and aware of their thoughts and emotions, you can develop greater self-awareness and a more positive outlook on life.

- **Better Physical Health:** In addition to the mental health benefits, mindfulness and meditation have also been shown to have positive physical health benefits, such as lower blood pressure and improved sleep.

- **Improved Relationships:** Mindfulness and meditation can help you develop a greater sense of empathy and compassion, leading to improved relationships and better communication skills. This can be especially beneficial for teenagers, who are often still developing their social and emotional skills.

Techniques for practicing mindfulness: deep breathing exercises and guided meditations

Mindfulness and meditation can be practiced in many ways, but the two standard techniques are deep breathing exercises and guided meditations.

Deep Breathing Exercises: Deep breathing exercises involve taking slow and also deep breaths and focusing on the sensation of the breath moving in and out of the body. This can help calm the mind and reduce feelings of stress and anxiety. You can practice deep breathing exercises anywhere, at any time, and for any length, making them a convenient and accessible way to incorporate mindfulness into your daily routines.

Guided Meditations: Guided meditation is another popular technique for practicing mindfulness. They involve listening to a recorded meditation or following along with a guided meditation app or video. Guided meditations often involve focusing on the breath, a mantra, or visualization and can be especially helpful if you are new to mindfulness and meditation.

Both deep breathing exercises and guided meditation are simple yet powerful techniques that can help you develop more significant focus, reduce stress, and improve your overall well-being. By incorporating these techniques into your daily routine, you can develop the skills and habits necessary to lead a more mindful and fulfilling life.

Tips for incorporating mindfulness into daily routines

Below are some tips for incorporating mindfulness into your daily routine:

Start Small: It can be overwhelming to fit a new habit into an already busy schedule. Start with just a few minutes each day and gradually increase your time practicing mindfulness.

Set a Routine: Try to practice mindfulness at the same time each day, whether in the morning or just before bed. This will help make it a habit and make it easier to remember to practice regularly.

Incorporate Mindfulness into Other Activities: Look for opportunities to be mindful throughout the day, such as brushing your teeth, taking a shower, or walking to school. Pay attention to your senses and the sensations in your body to stay present in the moment.

Use Reminders: Put up a reminder in your room or set a daily alert on your phone to help you remember to practice mindfulness.

Make It Fun: Mindfulness doesn't have to be serious or formal. Try to find a form of mindfulness that you enjoy, whether deep breathing exercises, guided meditations, or a mindfulness app.

Be Patient: Mindfulness takes time and practice to develop, so be patient and persistent. You have to keep in mind that it's a journey, not a destination.

Putting mindfulness into your daily routine can be a simple and effective way to reduce stress, improve focus and attention, and develop a greater sense of well-being.

The importance of regular physical activity

Physical exercise and movement are essential for overall health and well-being and play an important role in developing and maintaining executive functioning skills. Regular physical activity can help improve focus, attention, and mood and reduce stress and anxiety.

Physical exercise increases the flow of oxygen and nutrients to the brain, which can help improve cognitive function and enhance memory and learning. It also releases endorphins, the body's natural mood booster, helping to reduce feelings of stress and anxiety.

In addition to the physical benefits of exercise, regular physical activity can positively impact mental health. Exercise can help boost your self-esteem, reduce depression, and improve overall well-being.

By incorporating regular physical activity into your daily routine, you can enjoy the many benefits of exercise, both physically and mentally. Whether it's through structured exercise such as playing sports, taking a fitness class, or simply going for a walk, there are many ways to make physical activity a part of your daily routine.

Physical activity can improve cognitive function and mood in several ways:

Boosts Blood Flow to the Brain: Regular physical activity increases the flow of oxygen and nutrients to the brain, helping to improve cognitive function, enhance memory and learning, and reduce the risk of cognitive decline.

Increased Brain-Derived Neurotrophic Factor (BDNF): Exercise has been shown to increase levels of BDNF, a protein in the brain that helps to promote the growth of new brain cells and protect against age-related cognitive decline.

Reduces Stress and Anxiety: Exercise releases endorphins, the body's natural mood booster, which can help reduce feelings of stress and anxiety and improve overall mood.

Improves Self-Esteem and Confidence: Regular physical activity can help to boost self-esteem and confidence and increase feelings of self-worth

Games and puzzles

Games and puzzles can be a fun and effective way to challenge the brain and improve cognitive function. They can help stimulate the brain and keep it active, improving memory, attention, and overall cognitive ability.

Brain-stimulating games and puzzles come in many forms, including memory games, crosswords, Sudoku, and more. These games and puzzles challenge the brain differently and can help improve various cognitive skills, such as memory, problem-solving, and critical thinking.

Playing brain-stimulating games and puzzles can help improve cognitive function by engaging different brain parts. For example, memory games can help improve memory recall, while crosswords can help improve vocabulary and problem-solving skills.

In addition, these games and puzzles can also help to improve focus and attention. By challenging your brain and requiring focused attention, these games and puzzles can improve your ability to concentrate and stay focused, even in the face of distractions.

By incorporating brain-stimulating games and puzzles into your daily routine, you can enjoy the benefits of cognitive stimulation and improve your overall cognitive ability.

Effective study strategies include taking detailed notes, creating flashcards, summarizing information, and using mnemonic devices. These techniques help you organize and retain information and make studying more efficient and effective. It's also essential for you to have a consistent study routine and create a dedicated study space free of distractions. This can help students stay focused and motivated while studying.

Incorporating these effective studying strategies into a routine can help students improve their academic performance and achieve their goals. It's also essential to find what works best for each student, as everyone may have different learning styles and preferences.

Tips and Strategies for Studying Effectively

Taking Notes

Taking detailed and organized notes during lectures and reading can help you better understand and retain the information. This can include writing down key terms, concepts, and examples and summarizing information in your own words. Reviewing these notes regularly helps reinforce the information in your memory.

Creating Flashcards

Creating flashcards can be an effective way to study and retain information, especially for subjects that involve memorization, such as vocabulary or historical data. Writing and reviewing the information on the flashcards helps cement the information in your memory.

Using Mnemonic Devices

Mnemonic devices are memory aids that help you remember information by using a catchy phrase, acronym, or rhyme. For example, to remember the order of the planets in our solar system, students can use the mnemonic device "My Very Educated Mother Just Served Us Nine Pizzas" (Mercury, Venus, Earth, Mars, Jupiter, Saturn, Uranus, Neptune, Pluto).

You can effectively retain information and improve your academic performance by incorporating these study skills and memory techniques into your regular study routines.

The importance of developing social and emotional skills

Social and emotional learning (SEL) is developing skills related to emotions, relationships, and personal responsibility. These skills are essential for overall well-being, success in school and work, and positive relationships with others. Developing social and emotional skills, such as empathy, self-awareness, and communication, can help you navigate the challenges of growing up and lead happy, successful lives. It can also improve your relationships with friends and family and help them manage stress and emotions. SEL activities can include journaling, role-playing, group discussions, and other exercises that help you understand and express your emotions and develop positive relationships with others. By participating in SEL activities, you can learn valuable skills that will benefit them throughout your life.

Tips for incorporating social and emotional learning activities into daily routines

Incorporating social and emotional learning (SEL) activities into daily routines can help you develop essential skills and improve your well-being. Here are some tips for making SEL a regular part of daily life:

Set aside dedicated times: Allocate specific times during the day or week to participate in SEL activities, such as journaling or role-playing exercises. This can help make these activities a regular part of the routine.

Make it social: Participate in SEL activities with friends or family. This can provide opportunities for you to practice their social and emotional skills in a supportive environment.

Incorporate SEL into other activities: SEL activities can be incorporated into other aspects of daily life, such as taking a mindful walk or having a conversation about emotions with a friend.

Use of technology: Many digital resources, such as apps and websites, provide guided SEL activities and exercises. Using these resources can help make SEL a more accessible and convenient part of your daily routine.

By incorporating SEL activities into daily routines, you can develop essential skills that will benefit you throughout your life.

In this chapter, we discussed the importance of executive functioning and how it can be improved through various activities. We explored mindfulness and meditation practices, physical exercise and movement, brain-stimulating games and puzzles, study skills and memory techniques, and social and emotional learning activities. Each activity offers unique benefits for improving executive functioning, such as reducing stress, increasing focus and attention, and boosting memory.

Key Takeaways

- Practice mindfulness and meditation regularly: Regular mindfulness and meditation practices can help reduce stress, increase focus and attention, and improve overall well-being.
- Incorporate physical exercise into daily routines: Physical exercise and movement have improved cognitive function and mood.
- Lay brain-stimulating games and puzzles: Engaging in games and puzzles that challenge the brain can help improve cognitive function and memory.
- Use practical study skills and memory techniques: By using effective study skills and memory techniques, such as taking notes and using mnemonic devices, teenagers can improve their ability to retain information and perform well in school.
- Engage in social and emotional learning activities: Developing social and emotional skills such as empathy, self-awareness, and communication can help improve overall well-being and relationships with others.

Chapter 8: Workbook with Exercises to Apply the Executive Skills with Practice

Do you feel like you're always running out of time or struggling to stay organized? Do you find it hard to make decisions or solve problems effectively? If so, you're not alone! Organizational skills play a big role in our daily lives and can impact our success. Thankfully, these skills can be developed and strengthened with practice. In this chapter, I've put together a series of exercises and activities specifically designed for teens like you to improve your executive skills. Whether you're looking to manage your time, plan and organize your tasks, or improve your problem-solving abilities, this chapter has covered you. So, are you ready to take the first step toward mastering your executive skills? Let's get started.

Time management strategies (Worksheets):

Exercise 1: Time Audit

A time audit is a powerful tool that can help you take control of your time and become more mindful of how you're spending it. The goal is to help you identify areas where you can make changes to improve your time management. Here are some key steps to keep in mind when conducting a time audit.

- Write down all the activities you do in a day, including work, school, leisure, and self-care.

_____

_____

_____

_____

_____

_____

_____

_____

_____

_____

_____

_____

_____

_____

Estimate the amount of time spent on each activity.

Activity

_____

Time

_____

Activity

_____

Time

_____

Activity

_____

Time

_____

Activity

_____

Time

_____

Activity

_____

Time

_____

- Look at the total amount of time spent and identify activities that take up more time than you would like or that could be done more efficiently.

- Write down one strategy for each activity that could help you manage your time better.

Activity

_____

Strategy

_____

Activity

_____

Strategy

_____

Activity

_____

Strategy

_____

Activity

_____

Strategy

_____

Activity

_____

Strategy

_____

Activity

_____

Strategy

_____

Activity

_____

Strategy

_____

Activity

_____

Strategy

_____

Activity

_____

Strategy

Exercise 2: Prioritization

Prioritization is the key to making the most of your time and avoiding wasting it on less important tasks. By evaluating the importance and urgency of each task or activity, you can prioritize them and focus your attention and efforts on the most important ones.

By prioritizing your tasks, you can allocate your time and resources effectively, ensuring that you promptly complete the most important tasks. This will help you stay organized, focused, and on track, reducing the risk of missing deadlines, overlooking important tasks, or feeling overwhelmed. Follow these steps to help you prioritize your activities.

- Write down your daily tasks, both short-term and long-term.

  Long-term daily tasks

  _____

  _____

  _____

Short-term daily tasks

_____

_____

_____

_____

_____

_____

_____

_____

_____

_____

_____

_____

_____

_____

_____

_____

- Label each task as a high priority, medium priority, or low priority.

Hint: Write out the tasks and tick the appropriate priorities

_____

High   Medium   Low

_____

High   Medium   Low

_____

High   Medium   Low

_____

High   Medium   Low

_____

High   Medium   Low

_____

High   Medium   Low

Tip:

- Focus on completing high-priority tasks first, then move on to medium-priority tasks.

- Consider delegating or eliminating low-priority tasks.

Exercise 3: Setting Realistic Goals

Setting realistic goals is another important time management strategy that can help you stay focused and motivated. Goal setting involves defining what you want to achieve and setting targets to help you get there. By setting realistic goals, you can give yourself clear direction and a sense of purpose, making it easier for you to focus on what is truly important.

When setting goals, it's important to consider your strengths, weaknesses, and limitations and to choose goals that are both challenging and achievable. Setting unrealistic or overly ambitious goals can lead to frustration and disappointment while setting goals that are too easy can lead to boredom and lack of motivation. You can start by taking these steps.

- Write down your short-term and long-term goals.

Long-term goals

_____

_____

_____

_____

_____

_____

_____

_____

_____

_____

_____

_____

_____

_____

_____

_____

_____

_____

Short-term goals

_____

_____

_____

_____

_____

_____

_____

_____

_____

_____

_____

_____

_____

_____

_____

_____

_____

_____

_____

- Divide each goal into smaller, manageable activities.

Goal A: _____

Dividing **Goal A** into smaller, manageable activities

_____

_____

_____

_____

_____

_____

_____

_____

_____

_____

_____

_____

_____

_____

_____

Goal B: _____

Dividing **Goal B** into smaller, manageable activities

_____

_____

_____

_____

_____

_____

_____

_____

_____

_____

_____

_____

_____

_____

_____

_____

_____

_____

Goal C: _____

Dividing **Goal C** into smaller, manageable activities

_____

_____

_____

_____

_____

_____

_____

_____

_____

_____

_____

_____

_____

_____

_____

_____

_____

_____

_____

Goal D: _____

Dividing **Goal D** into smaller, manageable activities

_____

_____

_____

_____

_____

_____

_____

_____

_____

_____

_____

_____

_____

_____

_____

_____

_____

_____

_____

Goal E: _____

Dividing **Goal E** into smaller, manageable activities

_____

_____

_____

_____

_____

_____

_____

_____

_____

_____

_____

_____

_____

_____

_____

_____

_____

_____

_____

Goal F: _____

Dividing **Goal F** into smaller, manageable activities

_____

_____

_____

_____

_____

_____

_____

_____

_____

_____

_____

_____

_____

_____

_____

_____

_____

_____

_____

- Sort tasks according to their priority and urgency

Here, you use each quadrant to sort your tasks.

I'd go first:

Task A: I have a very urgent writing submission timeline.

Task B: I also need to go swimming.

Now, use the lower quadrant to fill yours.

Writing submission	Swimming
Urgent	Not Urgent

- Adjust your schedule to ensure you have enough time to work on your goals.

Exercise 4: Time Blocking

Time blocking is a technique that involves dividing your day into specific blocks of time, each dedicated to a specific task or activity. By using time blocking, you can better manage your time, prioritize your tasks, and avoid distractions and interruptions. One of the advantages of time blocking is that it helps you focus on one task at a time, reducing the risk of distractions and interruptions. This can improve your productivity and efficiency. Follow these steps.

- Plan your day by creating blocks of time for different activities.

Day 1

Activity

_____

Time

Activity

Time

Activity

Time

Activity

Time

Activity

Time

Activity

Time

_____

Activity

_____

Time

_____

Day 2

Activity

_____

Time

_____

Activity

_____

Time

_____

Activity

_____

Time

_____

Activity

_____

Time

_____

Activity

_____

Time

_____

Activity

_____

Time

_____

Activity

_____

Time

_____

Day 3

Activity

_____

Time

_____

Activity

_____

Time

_____

Activity

_____

Time

_____

Activity

_____

Time

_____

Activity

_____

Time

_____

Activity

_____

Time

_____

Activity

_____

Time

_____

Day 4

Activity

_____

Time

_____

Activity

_____

Time

_____

Activity

_____

Time

_____

Activity

_____

Time

_____

Activity

_____

Time

_____

Activity

_____

Time

_____

You can now start to create your time blocks based on your needs.

- Allocate specific times for work, school, leisure, and self-care.

- Set a timer to keep track of how long each activity takes.

- Evaluate and adjust your time blocks to ensure you use your time effectively.

Workbook

Exercise 5: Managing Distractions

Managing distractions is a critical part of effective time management. Distractions can come from a variety of sources, such as emails, phone notifications, social media, or interruptions from colleagues, and they can quickly derail your focus and productivity. Follow these steps to manage distractions.

- Identify your most common distractions, such as social media, texting, or television.

- Decide when and for how long you will allow yourself to be distracted.

- Use tools such as website blockers or phone apps to limit your access to distractions during work or study time.

- Find alternative activities during leisure time to avoid boredom and the temptation to be distracted.

Remember, it takes time and practice to develop effective time-management skills. Be patient with yourself and continue to try new tactics until you discover what works best for you.

Planning and organization techniques:

Exercise 1: To-Do List

A to-do list is a simple yet effective planning and organization technique that can help you stay on top of your tasks and achieve your goals.

Below are some points to follow when creating and using a to-do list:

- Pen down all the activities you need to complete each day, including work, school, leisure, and self-care.

- Sort tasks according to their priority and urgency.

- Write down the deadline for each task and allocate enough time to complete it.

- Cross off each task as you complete it, and update your list as needed.

Exercise 2: Calendaring

Calendaring is a powerful planning and organization technique that involves using a calendar to schedule tasks, appointments, and events.

The main goal of calendaring is to help you manage your time effectively and stay on top of your commitments.

Here are some key aspects of calendaring as a planning and organization technique:

- Write down important dates and events, such as birthdays, appointments, and deadlines

- Use your calendar to schedule these events and keep track of them

- Set reminders for important events to ensure you don't forget about them

- Review your calendar regularly to ensure you are on track and adjusting it as needed

Exercise 3: Note-Taking

Note-taking is a powerful organizational tool. It can be used in a variety of settings, including work, school, and your personal life. To help you stay organized, remember important information, and make the most of your time. Here are some steps when using notetaking as an organizational tool:

- Write down key information during lectures, meetings, or when reading

- Use abbreviations, symbols, and bullet points to simplify your notes and make them easier to read

- Review your notes regularly to reinforce your understanding of the information

- Use your notes as a reference when completing tasks related to the information

Exercise 4: Filing System

A filing system is a powerful tool for organizing and managing information. It can help you stay on top of your responsibilities and keep track of important information, such as documents, receipts, and notes. Follow these steps. Gather all your papers, including schoolwork, bills, and important documents.

- Label each paper and categorize it into folders

- Use a filing cabinet or file box to store your papers safely and securely

- Update your filing system regularly to ensure it remains organized and easy to use

Exercise 5: Timely Follow-Up

Timely follow-up is an important aspect of effective planning and organization. By following up on tasks and commitments on time, you can ensure that things get done on time and that you can stay on track with your goals. Here are some steps to follow.

- Write down any commitments you have made, such as completing a task or attending a meeting

- Set reminders for each commitment to make sure you follow up on them on time

- Review your commitments regularly to ensure that you are on track and adjust as needed

- Follow up on commitments promptly to show that you are responsible and dependable

These activities are a great starting point for improving your planning and organization skills. Practice using these techniques regularly, and you will see improvement over time.

Goal-setting and decision-making skills:

Exercise 1: SMART Goals

SMART goals are a useful tool for setting and achieving goals. By setting SMART goals, you can ensure that your goals are well-defined, attainable, and aligned with their overall objectives. Follow these steps.

- Write down your short-term and long-term goals

- Make sure each goal is Specific, Measurable, Attainable, Relevant, and Time-bound (SMART)

- Divide each goal into smaller, manageable activities

- Estimate the amount of time and resources required to execute each task

- Sort tasks according to their priority and urgency

Pros and cons analysis is a decision-making tool that helps you weigh the potential benefits and drawbacks of different options. By considering different options, individuals can make informed decisions and determine the best course of action for achieving their goals. Here are some steps to take:

- Write down a decision you need to make

- List the potential pros and cons of each option

- Evaluate the potential consequences of each option

- Choose the option that has the most benefits and the fewest drawbacks

- Write down a plan of action to implement your decision

Exercise 3: Mind Mapping

Mind mapping is a powerful visual tool that can help you brainstorm ideas, organize information, and make connections between different concepts. By creating a mind map, you can see the relationships between different ideas and develop a clear understanding of complex topics. Here is how to go about it:

- Write down a goal or problem you need to solve

- Draw a large circle in the center of a page and write the goal or problem

- Draw lines from the center circle to smaller circles and write down related ideas and possible solutions

- Evaluate each idea and choose the one you believe is the best solution

- Write down a plan of action to implement your solution

Exercise 4: Cost-Benefit Analysis

Cost-benefit analysis is a decision-making tool that helps you evaluate the costs and benefits of a potential action or investment. It involves weighing the costs of a particular course of action against the potential benefits to determine whether it is a worthwhile investment. Here is how to go about it:

- Write down a decision you need to make

- List the costs and benefits of each option

- Evaluate the financial and non-financial impact of each option

- Choose the option that provides the most benefits and the lowest cost

- Write down a plan of action to implement your decision

Exercise 5: Reflection and Review

Reflection and review is an important exercise in decision-making that allows you to assess your progress and make adjustments if needed. You need to take the time to reflect on what has been done, what has worked well, what could be improved, and what needs to be done next. Here is how to go about it:

- Reflect on a goal you have achieved or a decision you have made

- Write down what went well and what could have been improved

- Consider what you have learned from the experience and how you can apply it to future goals and decisions

- Review your goals and decisions regularly to track your progress and make necessary adjustments

By practicing these exercises, you can set achievable goals, make well-informed decisions, and continuously improve your goal-setting and decision-making skills.

Self-monitoring and self-evaluation:

Exercise 1: Self-Reflection

Self-reflection is a powerful self-monitoring and self-evaluation technique that helps you to become more aware of your thoughts, feelings, and behaviors. It involves taking the time to think about your actions, decisions, and experiences, and to evaluate your impact on your life and well-being. Follow these steps.

- Take time each day to reflect on your thoughts, feelings, and actions.

- Write down what went well and what could have been improved.

- Consider how your thoughts, feelings, and actions impacted your performance and well-being.

- Identify areas for improvement and plan to work on them.

Exercise 2: Tracking Progress

Tracking progress is an essential part of the self-monitoring and self-evaluation process. It allows you to see how far you've come, what's working well, and what needs improvement. Follow these steps.

- Choose a goal you want to achieve and write it down

- Break down goals into smaller, manageable tasks

- Track your progress toward each task and record it in a journal or spreadsheet

- Evaluate your progress regularly and adjust as needed

Exercise 3: Self-Assessment

Self-assessment is a valuable tool for self-monitoring and self-evaluation. It allows you to take stock of your skills, abilities, and behaviors, and to identify areas for improvement. Here is how to go about it:

- Choose a task or project you have completed

- Write down your strengths and weaknesses related to the task or project

- Evaluate your performance and consider what you could have done better

- Identify areas for improvement and plan to work on them

Exercise 4: Feedback-Seeking

Feedback-seeking is an important part of self-monitoring and self-evaluation. It involves actively seeking constructive feedback from others to give you a better understanding of your strengths and weaknesses, as well as identifying areas for improvement. By seeking feedback from others, you'll gain valuable insights into your performance. These steps will help you:

- Choose a task or project you have completed

- Ask someone you trust for feedback on your performance

- Listen to the feedback and write it down

- Evaluate your feedback and consider how you can use it to improve your performance

Problem-solving and critical thinking:

Exercise 1: Brainstorming

Brainstorming is a powerful problem-solving and critical-thinking technique that can help you to generate creative solutions to challenges. When you brainstorm, you bring together a group of people and encourage them to come up with as many ideas as possible without judging or criticizing any of the suggestions. Follow these steps to get started.

- Write down a problem or challenge you need to solve

- Gather a group of people or brainstorm on your own

- Write down as many potential solutions as possible, regardless of how ridiculous they appear

- Evaluate each solution and choose the one you believe best fits

- Write down a plan of action to implement your solution

Exercise 2: Root Cause Analysis

Root cause analysis helps to recognize the underlying causes of a problem or issue. This approach is often used in quality management, risk management, and continuous improvement initiatives. By identifying the root cause of a problem, you can prevent it from happening again in the future. Follow these steps.

- Write down a problem or challenge you need to solve

- Identify the underlying cause of the problem by asking "why" questions

- Write down the root cause of the problem and consider potential solutions

- Evaluate each solution and choose the one you believe best fits

- Write down a plan of action to implement your solution

Exercise 3: SWOT Analysis

SWOT analysis helps you to assess their strengths, weaknesses, opportunities, and threats (SWOT). By considering these factors, you can make informed decisions and develop a plan to achieve your goals. These steps will help you:

- Write down a problem or challenge you need to solve

- Write down the Strengths, Weaknesses, Opportunities, and Threats (SWOT) related to the problem

- Evaluate each aspect of the SWOT and consider potential solutions

- Choose a solution that maximizes your strengths, minimizes your weaknesses, takes advantage of opportunities, and minimizes threats

- Write down a plan of action to implement your solution

Exercise 4: Scenario Planning

Scenario planning is a useful technique for problem-solving and making informed decisions. You can create different potential scenarios for a given situation and consider the possible consequences of each. By thinking through various scenarios, you can identify potential challenges and opportunities, and plan ahead. When using scenario planning, it's important to keep in mind different variables and factors that may affect the outcome. This can help you make wise decisions and take proactive steps to reach your goals. Follow these steps:

- Write down a problem or challenge you need to solve

- Consider different scenarios that could result from each potential solution

- Evaluate each scenario's potential outcomes and choose the most desirable one

- Write a plan to implement your solution and prepare for potential scenarios

Practicing these exercises enables you to approach problems and challenges with creativity, critical thinking, and a well-planned solution.

In conclusion, by practicing these activities, you have taken an important step towards developing and improving your executive skills. Whether you're looking to manage your time more effectively, plan and organize your tasks, or become a better problem-solver, these exercises have provided you with all the tools and techniques you'll need.

Remember, executive skills are not developed overnight and require consistent effort and practice. But with patience and persistence, you will see significant improvements in your abilities. So, keep practicing, and keep striving towards your goals. You've got this.

Chapter 9: A Way Forward

Now that you have learned all about executive functioning skills, you'll understand that it's not only grown-ups who need to make use of them but teenagers too. There is no better time to learn and practice executive functioning skills than your teenage years; when your mind is supple, and your learned behaviors are still open to change. Becoming a master of executive functioning skills means developing tactical and smart ways to be composed, arrange, and harness your mind, talent, and skills. Executive functioning skills will help you stay focused, display self-control, plan and meet goals, and follow up or follow instructions, even when there are distractions and difficulties.

A lot of people develop executive functioning skills without knowing it. But here, you can consciously develop these skills, giving you a clearer understanding of growing and navigating life as a teenager. There are so many different paths to take, for example, college, theater schools, a career in media or tech, religion, business, and family. Yes, even if you do not attend college, you will still need executive functioning skills; they'll follow you wherever you go.

Now you have read every chapter in this book, you have all the resources you'll need to help you. However, there are still external resources out there that will be helpful to you. Being a teenager doesn't have to be characterized by making rash and irrational decisions. There is no fun in being disorganized, and self-improvement will always help you to feel more fulfilled and happier with life.

If there is one thing you have learned from reading this book, the world is complex, and you do not need to go through the world aimlessly. Make use of guidance, whether it be in the form of books such as this, or from an adult mentor or teacher.

As you have read earlier, these three brain functions need to be focused on if you want to develop executive function skills:

- Self-control (inhibitory)
- Mental (cognitive) flexibility
- Working memory

You'll likely require your self-control to be high almost all the time as it helps you preserve your discipline and integrity. With self-control, you can keep your head calm no matter how hard it gets, allowing you to focus on your goals rather than getting caught up in your distractions.

Mental flexibility and working memory are added benefits you can use to augment or complement your self-control. You can switch and focus from task to task with mental flexibility. Mental flexibility will also help you cope with drowning out distractions and difficulties.

Working memory is essential for everyday life. That way, you can grasp and take hold of schedules and details that you need to thrive. Working memory works with routines and priorities. With working memory, you can easily align with your routines; of course, it is best to only work on or with positive routines that build your character, academics, career, craft, and health. And even though you struggle with these features, cognitive flexibility, self-control, and working memory will help you deal with activities like planning, writing homework, deciding on a career, learning an instrument, scaling your grades, managing your time, organizing, speaking up, writing and noticing details. With these, you will feel less overwhelmed about your activities, helping you to carry out tasks with a calm and collected mind.

I bet you can grasp SMART goals; SMART goals are wonderful and can help you develop executive functioning skills quickly and efficiently. Using SMART to set your goals will always be useful.

S - Specific

M - Measurable

A - Achievable

R - Relevant

T - Time Bound

What do these mean?

These are specific guidelines for you when trying to fix or achieve your goals. Before achieving your goals, you must fix them, and while fixing them, you must make sure that your goals are:

Specific: your goals must be precise; suppose you set a goal like; I will get some strawberry cheesecake ice cream; it is much better than setting the goal; I will get some ice cream. When you get to the ice cream shop, there are so many flavors you can't think of which to go with. The absence of specific details for your goal sets you up for distraction, indecisiveness, indiscipline, and failure. But with specificity, you can direct your efforts towards your goals intentionally rather than always cutting corners. Do you understand the value of a specific goal now? With a specific goal, there is a direct location; like riding your bike to school. Without a specific location, it may take longer to get to a destination, if you get to one at all.

Reaching a goal is not taking a stroll; it is focusing on a particular point and making a direct effort to reach it. Much like archery, as you raise your bow and arrow, take a deep breath and prepare to fire. This means that you must keep your eye on the goal, regardless of what is going on around you. This requires self-control and mental flexibility, of course.

Measurable: ensure that your goals can be measured. This is because you will need to measure just how far you have come or how much you have achieved. You need to create milestones. Suppose it takes 290 steps to get to your backyard. Every 50th step is a milestone. Your milestone can be a gradual achievement, for example, going to the kitchen to make some cereal:

1. Getting up from your bed

2. Walking into the kitchen

3. Taking out a box of cereal

4. Taking out a jug of milk

5. Filling your bowl with cereal

6. Adding milk to the bowl

For the "eating cereal" goal, you must acknowledge each goal and the fact that you have achieved a fraction of it; it is a great way to encourage yourself.

If you go to college. You need to:

1. Go to high school

2. Finish high school

3. Take SAT exams

4. Write personal statements

5. Go for interviews

6. Pay necessary fees like application fees and the like.

Then you get admitted.

Breaking goals into small parts like that helps you to feel a greater sense of progress. That way, your goal does not seem too unrealistic or hard to reach anymore. You can also give more credit to yourself for winning all the small, individual battles along the way. It can help you fight imposter syndrome as you can keep track of the efforts you have put in along the way and reaffirm to yourself that you deserve to be where you are.

Achievable: Do not set goals that are too far-fetched. While it is great and fun to be ambitious, sometimes you just need to take it slow and steady, one step at a time. Set goals with pace.

"I am going to build the next big social media app,"

But what if you do not know software engineering, engineering, or coding languages?

You must start with the basic stuff like learning about software engineering, project management, and all the other factors that go into creating an app. There is a reason for the saying: "Rome wasn't built in a day".

Not even the best structure can be built in a day. You need to focus on the important structural details, so you don't get lost in the idealistic bigger picture and become overwhelmed. As we have already learned, becoming overwhelmed only ends up being a hindrance that can derail your goals if you are not careful.

Relevance: Your goal must be relevant. Your goals must be relatable to you. Your goal should reflect the following:

- Current time frame
- Your values
- Accessible technology
- Your subsequent goals.

If your goals lack relevance to your life or interests, then the likelihood is you will lose the motivation to pursue them. The same can be said for whether the technology required to carry out your goal is accessible to you. If not, you will struggle to achieve what you initially set out to achieve.

Time-bound: Make sure that your goals have set deadlines. This will help to keep you on your feet so that you can ensure that you are on track. Suppose you have an essay to put in soon, let's say you have three days. You will be more diligent than you would have been if you had a thirty-day deadline. Because you are up against time, you'll think of better solutions and be more proactive. Set time frames and make sure to stick to them.

Executive function skills will continue to be essential for you to gain independence, improve your critical thinking skills, follow through with goals, and look ahead to your future.

Remember, you are almost an adult. All adults were once teenagers like you. Therefore, now is the time to learn these premium skills that will help you on the path to becoming a happy and successful adult. Executive functioning skills will be noticeable in your everyday life, from planning, to time management, to academics.

These skills are vital for important factors in your life such as keeping a job, maintaining relationships, and managing your finances. It is also important that you monitor short and long-term goals. Self-monitoring is an essential skill for every teenager to master, especially if they are trying to be conscious of their achievements and lifestyle.

If you have already started practicing and are struggling to notice any changes, do not worry. Executive functioning skills take time to master. If you are experiencing difficulties with practicing, it is normal, after all, there is a lot to work on.

Thankfully, there are so many great ways to help you improve. The bottom line is that you do have executive functioning skills. It is also beneficial to talk about this with your parents and to discuss what exactly you are trying to do. Your parents will likely be willing to help, as it is an effort toward your personal development.

Taking Further Steps

If you have gotten through all the resources in this book and would like to further your practice, there are more ways that you can excel. There are tons of books to read, including 'Brain Rules' by John Medina. Another excellent book on the topic is, 'Becoming Better Grown-ups: Rediscovering What Matters and Remembering How to Fly' by Brad Montague.

Becoming a better adult doesn't have to be boring, you can also learn from movies. Disney's 'Inside Out' is a great movie, centering around the complexities of the human mind in a fun, digestible way. In the movie, you get to see the main character Riley try to live and manage her four emotions after experiencing some personal trauma. The movie is thought-provoking and therapeutic to watch, offering a unique perspective on the challenges of mental health and how to overcome the toughest aspects of it.

While you try to put all your effort into self-improvement, you should also never forget the power of friendship and companionship. Friends can be of great help; they can be the tiny push you need or the giant pillar you can lean on.

However, you must make sure that you and your friends have values that align. It is never going to be helpful if you have conflicting ideas and principles. You do not have to have common goals, but common values are very important to have or share.

There is a simple exercise for this chapter. Write out fifteen things you have learned from this book in your journal or diary, a sticky note, or a piece of paper. Cut it out and then keep it over your door or your mirror. Keep it somewhere where you will be able to see it frequently. This way it will be difficult to lose track of the improvements that you intend to start making.

Conclusion

The journey of developing your executive functioning skills is a rewarding one. Whether you struggled with organization, planning, or time management or wanted to improve your cognitive skills, you have now gained a deeper understanding of the importance of executive functioning and how to develop these skills. Following the strategies and activities outlined in this book, you have taken a bold step toward unlocking your full potential.

This book provides a comprehensive overview of executive functioning and its importance in the lives of teens. This book covers a range of critical topics, from understanding the key components of executive functioning and how they impact daily life to identifying and assessing executive functioning deficits and learning strategies to improve these skills. By incorporating the strategies and activities outlined in this book, you can develop your executive functioning skills and reach your full potential.

The benefits of improved executive functioning skills are evident. You will have better academic success, more effective time management, and stronger social relationships. Improved executive functioning skills will help you achieve your goals and become the best version of yourself.

In conclusion, it is very important to understand that executive functioning is not a fixed trait but something that can be developed and improved with practice. The key to success is to be persistent and consistent in your efforts. As you continue to apply the strategies and activities in your daily life, you will begin to see improvement in your cognitive skills. Remember that developing your executive functioning skills takes time and patience, but the result will be worth it.

In closing, I hope this book has helped guide you toward improved executive functioning skills. I am confident that the strategies and activities outlined in this book will help you achieve your goals, and I wish you the best of luck on your journey toward success. Remember to keep practicing and applying what you have learned, and always strive towards your full potential.

RANDOM NOTES & WORKBOOK PARTS

Made in United States
Troutdale, OR
12/29/2023

16528632R00106